Evidence of Rain

Evidence of Rain

poems

Carol Rucks

NODIN PRESS

ACKNOWLEDGEMENTS
Grateful acknowledgment is given to the editors of the publications where some of these poems have previously appeared, often in different versions: "Soup," *West Branch*; "Venice," *Loonfeather*; "Robbery," *Poetry Bone*; "Ray Bradbury Standing," *Portage*; "Tourist," *Colere*; "A Change of Address," *Abraxas*; "Shadow" and "May," *Sidewalks Online*; "Discovering Periwinkle," *Re-Imagining*; "A Vacation Resembling Dying," *Dust and Fire*; "To a Stranger on the Greyhound Bus," *Buffalo Bones*; "Father," *The Northern Reader*.

And a special thanks to Norton Stillman for his openness and generosity, to Dara Syrkin for her keen editor's eye, and to John Toren, book designer. Many thanks to the good teachers and fellow writers who have helped and inspired, especially Roseann Lloyd, Tom Heie, Thomas Smith, Mike Rollin, and Jude Nutter. Thanks to my writers' group: June Blumenson, Marlene Jezierski, Kathe Warneke, and Sharon Soderlund. I am also grateful for the assistance and readership from Judy Treise.

Design: John Toren

Cover photo copyright: Andreiuc88 | dreamstime.com

ISBN: 978-1-935666-69-1

  Library of Congress Cataloging-in-Publication Data
  Rucks, Carol.
  [Poems. Selections]
  Evidence of Rain : poems / Carol Rucks.
  pages cm
  ISBN 978-1-935666-69-1
  I. Title.
  PS3618.U335A6 2014
  811'.6--dc23
                              2014031575

Nodin Press
5114 Cedar Lake Road,
Minneap0lis, MN 55416

For my parents

Nature loves to hide. It rests by changing.

– Heraclitus

Contents

II

III

I

FABLE

In the arbor where we live
jackrabbits speak softly about the price
of life, saying each day
must be paid out in silver or gold.
The long grass must be worked on,
the sisters spoken to.
Good friends will marry
woodcutters, and move away.
It is futile to prepare
for the future, except to eat well
and sleep soundly under the garden of stars.
People and animals will come and go
in a whisper, like rain rolling in
and rolling away.
To keep the homestead full of life,
water all of the trees.

IMAGINING THE MOURNING DOVES

I swear I heard them suddenly
last night as I tried to sleep.
It was ten below and the furnace
mumbled to the wind.
A gentleness brushed against
the glass, a plea, a flash
of light along the window.

GRAY UNDERWEAR

Father came to visit last night
wearing a white T-shirt and gray underwear.
He roamed the house, checking
the voracity of electrical outlets,
the power of fans.
He looked for dust, dirt,
the naked crumbs under everything.
And he should know;
he lives in that world.
He seemed contented, dressed
inappropriately, unshaven
and groggy, stumbling
through the cloud of my dream.

ROME

We'll miss the man
in black, pointy shoes
selling paper cones of green olives
from a metal vendor stand.
And also, the handsome one
we saw every day strolling by
in pinstriped trousers,
smelling of garlic and poverty.

ROBBERY

I got caught stealing stockings and a pair of elegant shoes
from a shop on Nicollet Avenue.
I was supposed to meet my husband at a café there,
to drink glasses of Burgundy wine.
The boys caught me, red-handed, so I gave the items back.
I told them I'd never stolen anything before, but it's a lie.
I lifted girlfriends from my sisters and boyfriends
from my brothers. I took the gold from the sun
and buried it in the garden. I seized the attention
and energy of younger men, and left them whimpering.
I pilfered stardust, and then put it back.
I stole compliments, and waved them away.
As a child, I slipped into the neighbor's house
to look at rooms of fine furniture, test
the neatly made beds. Afterward,
I palmed two olives from the refrigerator door.

Winter Orphanage

The forest of loneliness
is where we'll live.
Winter will find us, remember
our exact address.
Something's rattling the front door now,
perhaps a sentry in uniform
with uncertain news.
We'll miss our parents most.
Their absence will tear at us
like the yellowed linoleum floor,
the cracks in the ceiling.
And even the devil, the wind,
will forget us.

FEAR OF NOVEMBER

These yellow skies
of stunned trees, maples and oaks,
float their paper wigs
as the dead return.
The old ones visit us in late October,
or so we think,
in our half-frightened masks,
our anxieties of the dark.
We fear being left in a colorless world
without end, to be separated
from the sun and from love,
the wind at our backs
kicking us sideways from the west,
the snow polishing our faces.

RAIN

The day he made up his mind
to fall in love with someone
else,
I took my fate back.

The sky trembled,
revealing islands of blue
colors. I rushed
to the window to hear
the song of water.

A Vacation Resembling Dying

In another country I fell away
from the memory of my old life.
I still loved my husband
and all of his shadows,
but the phone wouldn't reach him,
the ringing wouldn't stop.
A voice that answered once
could have been an angel,
but it wasn't him.
I drifted in and out of memory
from my hilltop dwelling,
thinking of our home, garden,
and place on earth.
My new life was good too—
I had money to spend
that came out of nowhere.
There were friends, coffee shops, exotic trees,
all felt peaceful and free,
and I cried for no one.

FLYING DREAM

Floating above the trees,
I used my eyes.
I saw lush trees and flowers,
the births of new animals.

Floating above the houses,
I used my ears.
I heard the full music
of food and drink inside open rooms.

Floating above the river,
I used my tongue.
I tasted the green water
of the broad canal, the boats
sluicing through the bitter tea
and fog of heavy air.

IRELAND

In Ireland, everything glowed
in black and white.
Even your face looked colorless.
A funeral began, people milled
near the hearse, a cemetery loomed
in front of us.
Young boys sang their hearts out,
putting their childhoods behind them.
We wandered down a country lane
as music darkened the trees.

WHITEFISH LAKE

We enter the gold water
and see our own legs
at the depth of two feet,
three feet.

We enter the honey
completely then,
and forget we have bodies.

VENICE

Sleeping next to the blondest sister
I had a dream.
We crawled onto the roofs of Venice
where white gulls strutted
and the green water below called to us.

It was only the whiff of spring
from the open window, trees waking up,
and the new roots of violets.

Our dolls slept with us,
cold and eyeless,
aching to become light.

I followed her over the red-tiled roofs,
looking for clues from the crowd below.
Churches filled up, shops opened,
and the rotted bases of buildings
showed their white stain.

It wasn't my sister, but a man I used to love,
walking the crumbling avenues with me.
I slipped into the Grand Canal
and slowly swam away.

THE TULIP REPORT

A yellow one
trimmed in pink
held a green interior.

Another, painted lipstick
red and blue, faded
beneath a white sheen.

The strange apricot one
glowed lemon chiffon
deep inside.

Flowers are like people becoming
more complex
as they possess their passions,
oranges and reds.

The white tulip, traced with yellow
lace, appears both masculine
and feminine under blue-
gray skies.

MAY

We watch the cardinal's nest
quietly, waiting to make our plans.
The wild columbine opens
green and gray shoots.
We dig in, pull out a few weeds,
a few dead friendships.
Sunlight trapped in wet maple leaves
glows red-yellow.
The new grass sprouts its seed
in a corridor of pale rain,
and diamonds gleam on the sidewalk.

THE MOMENT

At the moment of death
when the bills have all been paid
and the taste of rain falls
into our mouths,
the gods will take us north
beyond the land of honey and sun.
We will miss our chance at love,
its mystery and dance.
We will miss the garden
and its music.
The colors of the world will fill
our eyes with calm,
and green clouds
will drift into blue
clouds.

THE VISITOR

For the visitor
lights of the city
shine like broken
glass. The night alley
perspires beads, nerves
held in all the way
from a faraway country,
are let go.
He sleeps on the floor,
watches for mice and insects.
This is not what he expected.
He dreams of distant beaches,
green landscapes.
The hand at his neck
is his own hand,
holding the bed sheet
like a wave of water.
He came to study
in America,
lie down in wealth and comfort.
At dusk there is a strange rattling
of languages—
a man shouting
in his sleep.

SHADOW

There are no shadows like this shadow,
no parade of trees
or plain brown birds who sing early
in Spanish arias.
No cream hibiscus where I live.

Up there, the oatmeal skies
drop soot from automobiles
on crust of ice,
making snowbanks rocky-road.

Blue sky scares me
and the yellow roses startle
me out of a slumber, a frozen depth.
I walk the halls of Hades in my dreams
and the devil hands me a snow shovel.

In the center of this town
a patch of green cacti warms in the sun.
Lavender petals of jacaranda fall on our heads.
We drink these colors
dry in one swallow
in the hungry shadow of lavender trees.

ELEVEN KINDS OF SNOW

The Inuit never walked on the kinds we've got:

The blackened mountains painted with car exhaust

The peanut brittle lumps of yellow melt at outdoor faucets

The hard-crusted blankets to levitate on

The rolled out, softened mix of early morning bread dough

The sanded over, sprinkled with cinnamon snow

The hard pack of cigarettes and litter

The footprints of sneaker designs at bus stops

The delicate patch of sparrow hatch marks

The heavy and sticky snowman-ready cotton

The soft hail of white couscous

And the light, airborne crystals of new sugar

BLANKET OF NEW SNOW

A fresh hatch of snow
like an animal of pure beginnings
lays over the yard without a wrinkle
or crack, a swoop of white
edifice, a solid breath
unfurls as an object of cold
and stunning silence
across the gardens and under
pine trees, seamless, sexless,
without footprints or tracks.

THINKING OF WINTER IN THE MIDDLE OF JULY

At daybreak
the sun came up quickly
and drew sweat across my face.
I wanted a cooler bed,
the silence and death
of a dark house.
I heard the garbage collectors
scrambling at their work.
A strong wind funneled aluminum
cans down the alley,
dragging the scrape of metal
against concrete, like the sound
of someone out alone
shoveling snow.

SUNRISE ON FAIRMOUNT STREET

The last dirty ice
mountains shrink in place.

Melt and twigs
trickle into the grate.

Cardinals flit. Squirrels scuffle
around the base of an elm tree.

The sun climbs the hill
of the brown and gray garage roofs.

We fill our lungs with something new:
part gasoline fumes, part April air.

Bike riders dodge beer cans,
rotting bags, and pockets of mud.

Canada geese test the landing strip
in front of the MacKay Envelope Factory.

Behind us, the steady scrape of leaves and dust
breaks the darkness of a hundred cold days.

TALKING TO THE MOON

Today, I saw the moon
slip through the clouds.
It peered forward
on Elm Street, illuminating
dog walkers in the snow.
I wanted to stare,
to see the light that measures time.
I waited, holding my eyes steady.
Birds fluttered in the trees,
the mailman stumbled by.
For a moment,
the sky made room for us.
I saw the pale body
encircled
by a living shroud,
before the clouds covered us
in a kind of silence.

NIGHT BLINDNESS

He came to love the darkness
of rain clouds and crows,
the slanted light behind the trees
at nine in the evening.
His face betrayed him
one night in the mirror,
yellow patches on his skin
resembled the lunar surface.
He gave up his hat, his umbrella
and cane. He gave up the garden walks
and the noise of the theater.
In the life of the tavern
he learned to fit inside the shadows.
The rounded face of the moon
was the only woman he loved.

LOOKING FOR ANCESTORS

Though we have traveled
deeply into the center
of nowhere, we don't know
what country it was called,
which fields were Polish
or German, what crops
wheat or rye.
We have postcards
from our grandmothers
of saints and kings, maps
of provinces in two languages.
The borders were flattened
by the battles of peasant-slaves.
By the looks of the abandoned
graves, they left in a hurry, and never
came back. Only the fields
remember them, the silhouettes
of great trees.

Soup

The oldest woman in Poland fed us a bowl of soup
with little people floating on top.
She fattened us on dumplings and beefsteak
and asked us to hide behind an apron.

We were scared, but never said a word
through Lublin and Deblin, where a shadow fell low,
swallowing up the colors of the field.

White cranes fluttered in the grass.
We watched them carefully,
afraid their silent shapes might never reach the sky.

In the heart of Europe, men wore thin, dirty clothes
and pushed their bodies into work.
Their hands were the color of potatoes.

II

THE SADNESS OF AUGUST

In the three-ring circus
called childhood,
we escaped manners and parents
by running circles around the neighbors
with our black dog.
Sneaking out of the attic window
late at night, we slid down the carport
poles on a search
and destroy mission, to steal
cigarettes, explore empty
houses and schools.
We were caught and harshly sentenced
to our half-acre of guilt
and dull grass
in the warmest month of the year.

NIGHT FLOWERS

In a crowded room of dressers and beds,
a dirty curtain opened to the street light.
I heard my father creep
up the steps, crawling
over clothes, dolls, and magazines.
He came to find us, tickle us drunk
with silliness or tenderness, either way
his whiskers rubbed our faces
hard, until we laughed and cried.

Tonight he woke us to cook
his dinner, bring the meat and salad
to his door. His smoke
filled our lungs and caught us dreaming.

WINTER

At the feeder one lone bird
pecks all day
at a few odd seeds and crumbs.
This will stoke him
for now, through sleet
and penetrating wind.
The sticky frost
on bushes and trees
burns his hunger
to memory.

THE KITCHEN

In the green kitchen with its ancient clock,
a window exposed the carport, I could feel the driveway
darken under the dream of snow,
a stand of jack pine and bicycles in the yard.
In the kitchen I learned the luxury of coffee,
and tasted that necessity, woke up to it.
I'd sit with my parents to discuss the meaning of the day.
Being one of the older children,
I was privileged in this way to sit and get along
while they seemed to like each other.
There was a drawer for napkins, a drawer for scissors,
and something masculine hidden in another drawer
with greasy tools, nails, hammers, all
belonging in the basement workshop.
Later, other things appeared, gin or beer,
olives in wine glasses, oysters, all adult items
intended for disorder. In the green kitchen
with its ancient clock, the evening loosened
its drawstrings. By midnight, my mother
opened her blouse to him, while I
sat in the next room, silent and tired.

PHOTOGRAPH IN NOVEMBER

We are eager children waiting to eat
in a colorful room with low lights.
We say little and hand food
over the luminous tablecloth.

Words will be swallowed with Grandma's soup,
butter tendered by mother's nervous eyes.
We're worried that our unmatched dishes
will make Grandma laugh.
It's lunchtime on a Saturday.
Father's gone again.
The meager prayer
we whisper
will shiver like a lie.

THE TUNNEL DREAM

for Joel

My brother guides me
through the attic, pushes the door
to a tunnel. We crawl in,
drop down to another level.
This is a dream I move through
every five years.
The tunnel takes us across
a mild tremor of chaos,
as we drag ourselves
over metal and wood,
and are emptied into a room.
There, we find Christmas
ornaments wrapped in cellophane,
bundles of love letters,
unbroken toys.

HE WAS A BOAT

Inside the black stairwell at the river
he climbed into ordinary hours,
taking a few solid steps
inside the sunbeam of his raft.

In sleep, he couldn't slumber,
in sex, he couldn't stop.
On land, he walked a little like a duck.

He was a sail and a rudder,
possessing a singular oar
in the belly of his hull.

Sadness wells up
inside the chest of a man
becoming God on the water.

He looked for glowing clouds
over the waves, but couldn't touch
them. He became the silver light
flickering there.

FATHER

I looked at you through the leaded glass of history.
I saw you in the grassy banks of church yards,
where red-faced Englishmen strolled the flowered grounds.
I called you from a bar in Galway, toasted
the dark pint to you.
I walked to Carnival, and slept with the poor,
sending you letters from Munich and Kassel.
I tried to pin you down on love and philosophy,
but this conflicted ancestry got in the way
with its etiquettes, arches and rains.
Behind each garden folly
a project could begin again— ship building,
map drawing, the plotting of corridors—
all the plans to begin and abandon,
so many women, drinks, waterways to explore.
After my first trip through Europe, I waited
for you at the Plainfield Bar and Bowl.
You never showed up.

FATHER II

When Father was alive,
he followed orders from the wind.
He drove his motorcycle through the late-night
side roads, taverns, and parking lots.
On Sundays he slumbered late
under heaven's blue eye.
We attended all seven
of the lonely sacraments.

But Father is still here, famished
for gin and steak,
arguing with the UPS driver,
and the radio, the television.
He's eating with his mouth open,
his wild fork stabs the air.

LIGHTNING

It's fatal to love him
and all the fog and cloud that go with him.
Even sitting close is bad luck
because the light he gives off
gets stuck in your eyes,
and the rain won't come.
I've been looking toward him, wishing
I could touch his imperfect shoulder,
cover up the boredom of a long summer day.
He's dragged out the polished
bicycle from the shed,
and his legs look healthy, ready to roll.
He's going now,
off to light up the sky,
blinding everyone in his path
with his electric and luminous love.

MICHELANGELO

The ribs on his chest
stood out like a thin girl's.
His face was too white,
his fingers, gray.
The language he spoke
was a city language of sidewalks
and dark cafés.
I try to remember him:
the caramel eyes, the great height.
His lanky brown hair
smelled like green apples
each time we kissed.

FATHER III

He's fallen off to sleep
for the last time.

I realize he's gone. Panic
slips into my mouth.

What he gave me I burned
up twice, once with anger,
once with doubt.

A silence enters me softly,
like a closed door,
or a cleaned-out closet.

His pillow is as dark
as a wrinkled star.

FATHER IV

The September light
flickers on the cherry tree.
Darkness takes its turn
with sun.

A scarlet bush fills up
with sparrows,
holds the quiet of the dead,
lacy leaves.

Father, I miss
what I caught a glimpse of:
the determination behind the work
of plastering walls,
sweeping out dusty basements,
the notes of tenderness
inside the harsh words.

TOURIST

I don't want to be a tourist
to someone else's suffering,
to crawl inside the heartache
and tears behind each portico
separating your anguish from mine.

You kneel before the cross
and the Mary
and the Joseph
because you know them well,
you speak their language.
I'm only a visitor, moving through time
zones of silence and fog,
without leaving a footprint.

I don't belong in this doorway,
this churchyard, this plot of cacti,
though I love the colors of the trees,
and I'm picking up the phrasing of the wind,
the humbleness of dust.

THE WEDDING PHOTOGRAPH

In spring bloom, near the shingled house,
they looked like dolls on a layered cake,
both virgins,
both crazy about each other,
and motorcycles, movies, Glen Miller.

They stood outside the house
shoulder to shoulder,
Father's gray suit pressing into the purity
of Mother's white linen.
She held him sideways
with a thin, freckled arm.

Years later,
Father would stumble in
from an evening out alone,
watch television from his chair.
He would throw a shoe
at any kid
who came between him and Johnny Carson.

Mother found her place
on the couch,
away from cooking, cleaning,
and children.

They never talked
or touched,
but laughed together at the moving gray screen,
where they still found a haven.

FATHER V

He died catching up
on sleep and love.
He gave away his motorcycles,
but kept the fuel
in the bottom drawer.

His blond dresser and bed,
a simple cut from 1962,
held a scent of mystery
and need.

We think we hear him now
lumbering in the hallway
as the dawn opens,
his hand reaches out
for a bird
in the wallpaper.

FATHER VI

In their bedroom
long ago, the family
cedar chest rested
near the blond, wooden bed
where they slept.
She kept her clothes in half
of the large closet,
her name written in institutional
marker on each blouse.
His starched shirts, smelling of Old Spice,
hung elegantly in a row.

As a child, I had a nightmare,
and went to him in the dark.
He let me sleep between them
in the warm, white sheets.
Under his breath, his arm around me,
the clock went silent.

RED LIPSTICK

She played the piano wildly
without sheet music,
because the pages were torn, or falling to pieces.
My mother used her whole body for the song,
riding that horse without a saddle.

She appears to me in red lipstick, pale skin,
her eyes a forest of muted green.
Her movements were sensual and slow,
even if the screen door slammed,
and the dog ran away.
She carried her babies on a graceful hip.

Her sweaters were worn tight, not flashy
but glamorous. She looked like a movie star,
circa 1942. Her legs were long and thin.
She was part Rita Hayworth,
part Lucille Ball.

As one of us, she played kitchen games—
Yahtzee, He Said She Said, or Hangman.
We watched "American Bandstand"
after making the trudge home, our arms full of books.
She played Mass with us, giving out hunks
of Wonderbread from Melmac plates.

Though she was kind, she could not guide us
over the rough parts, or tell us which people to avoid.
Her sensitivities created doubts, her mind hesitated
and traveled into secret detours.

She cooked a plate of eggs, not quite done.
She dusted under the bed, not really clean.
She stopped driving and shopping
to curl up on the sofa like an old cat.

Crooning on the radio,
Nat King Cole rolled out lazy summer days.
We sometimes put on swim suits together,
spread a blanket over the grass.
When the sun warmed us enough,
we rubbed baby oil on each other
and cooked in the heat like sisters.

Father VII

Once, in high school,
I came home later than I promised
after driving around with friends,
gliding through all the yellow lights.

We were out looking for boys
in the warm, spring night,
cruising through the high school
parking lot, the open turnaround
at the Dairy Queen, past downtown,
over the river and back.

When I came home at last,
he was on the sofa, half- asleep
in striped pajamas.
The fear in my hand
rattled the metal door knob.

He got up suddenly, looked me over.
I blurted out everything in a flurry—
the boys, the bottle of Spanada,
the midnight drive through town.

He stood there, motionless,
staring at the wall.
And then he turned to me and said,
because you were so honest with me
I am not going to punish you.

SURPRISES

When I brushed away the cobwebs
in the basement,
a small moth flew out.
It seemed as amazed as I was,
and delighted with the gift,
as when you arrived to greet me
at the train station
wearing a new blue shirt,
and clutching a single rose
in your hand.

TO A STRANGER ON THE GREYHOUND BUS

I met you, Mary Williams,
and we sat together in the night of rugged trees.
An ashen wind lapped against the back-drop
of old farmhouses.

We rode with the unknown others
while muffled lights and cities
faded behind like ghosts.

The odor of bus disinfectant mixed strangely
with the twice-breathed air.

We heard the scratch and boom
of someone's music,
the coagulated voices stuttering
every reverent thought and dream.

I wish you well, Mary Williams,
as you travel to your lost hometown
to meet your father on his deathbed,
pushing back the darkness and the long road.

THE END OF FEBRUARY

A dusting of light snow
falls on my heartache. I slept

late, and rumbled through a dozen dreams.
He didn't say goodbye and stunned me to the bone.

A battalion of crows sift the morning sugar,
erasing human footprints.

The crows are messengers
from the other world, couriers of bad news.

I tried to guess the shape of his leaving
by measuring close, watching the sky.

Silence first, then blackness,
and new snow.

FEAR

The hard breath of the frost
glistens on the grass.
A few birds flutter in the tree.
The sun makes us doubt
that our names are written on both sides
of the maple leaf,
growing in, and floating out.
Someone, behind the garage
with a raised hand,
is waiting to have a word
with us.

MONSTERS

Every one of us has a monster
inside their body
of some odd shape and size.
They fight the weight of life
for us, in different ways.
Some short change their employees.
Others wear down family
life, allowing us to bicker
over laundry.
Even the most calm, the most
forgiving, hold the centaur
in their eyes, becoming ruthless
when the head is turned,
to curse your backside.
At night, in darkened beds,
these creatures sleep
just as hard as we do.

FREUD

after Lucille Clifton

I began with stinginess.
I was a child with a stubborn mind.
My heart longed for clarification.
My red heart longed for peace.
In the middle of the story my daughter betrayed me.
I am not Carl Jung.
I did not define the meaning of churning water.
How did I end up here, sitting stiffly in a wooden chair,
while people labor all around me?
I am left with my dignity only.
I am Sigmund Freud.

THE CERTAINTY OF DREAMS

Don't fall into the beauty and become the river.
Don't let the open spaces soothe your mind.
Beware of the dangers of each adventure.
Don't be mesmerized by the refuge of silence.
Every lonely place has its secret danger.
The bigger the thrill, the more vulnerable one is.
Gravity is not our friend.
Don't fall in love with the colors of a storm.
Death is always here, no matter the weather.
Every cloud and rainstorm can destroy something.

APRIL RAIN

A thousand raindrops tap
the dirty window pane.
Father is dying in his white bed,
Mother is sleeping with her black cat.

And sandwiched for a time
between the silver lining of a cloud
and the darkness of a sparrow's wing,
a moment of happiness shivers
through the wet lilacs.

The red maple stands like an uncle
against the skyline,
giving away green money.

Every time I try to grasp
this beauty with my hands,
a few more clouds sail in from the west,
and settle like lawn chairs
on damp grass.

FINDING HER

When I turned twenty-four
her personality disappeared.
I visited from the city and tried
to talk to her. She couldn't hold on,
but laughed and laughed at clouds
rolling by, at late-night television, even
the evening prayers of the archbishop.
Her head rolled back, her mouth
opened wide, she seemed to enjoy
slipping into colors and fog.
In the morning I looked again
in the backyard rabbit hutch,
around the neighbor's swing set,
trudging through the sandbox
beneath the pine trees.
I began my fantasy
of finding her.

III

LIFE ON EARTH

Starlings,
beauties that will not last,
huddle around the chimney steam.
They suffer each separation
of breast and heat.

I hear in their murmurings to the pale sun
almost a song of praise.
They tease each other with a shove,
muscling in, and showing off.

They seem to love this earth, this heaven.
Perhaps I have waited long enough to pray.
Now, I am comforted
by picking up a branch of evergreen.

AFTERMATH

Birdsong on a cool morning
feeds the green light of the trees.
Pleasure becomes mist in the open
window of last night's dream:
old boyfriend, old apartment, old city.
His caramel eyes and hair,
the rich voice calls me in.
I love the cliff of his shoulders,
the almost hairless chest.
As a grown man he becomes
calm and touchable,
living quietly in the time
of a second emotion.

A CHANGE OF ADDRESS

Where there was a stream, there is a path of stones.
Where there was a lake, a silver freeway.
Here spruce grow
thirty feet above the planking of the house,
drop cones like rain
on warm asphalt,
in love with the impossible.

I Chased You Down

Because I wanted to discover
a different kind of love,
I chased you down hallways of Melmac,
and kitchens of glass,
I kept you running down a dark tunnel
smelling of warm earth, worked you under
a bridge of wooden statuary. There
in the evening, before you awoke, I dove
toward cover in a ballroom full of refrigerators,
past water heaters on parade, to breathe in factory air
with you, forgetting Mother's love and its gentleness,
forgetting Father's love and its sternness.
I brought you back to the river's edge with kisses and toast,
where the waves moved in tandem with fish.
The night became electric, streaked with light,
and the rain began to taste like the fragrant body
of the sea.

GARDENING

The world of small things being born
ticks with love, pain, and triumph.
I rake out the bark and leaves,
the dead must go.
I return with a bucket of raindrops,
the memory of jack-in-the-pulpit.
The trillium's white dream
restores best in the morning.
If a seed refuses to beat like a heart,
there's a twinge in the left
side of my body, a spasm
of time fading out.
I pull on the black, plastic shoes,
go out into the mud.
I work my fingers deep,
while the wind takes me.
The sun is my garden.

THE GOLDENROD

The vivacity of the goldenrod
as it bends into the sun
with firm resolve
makes me wonder if I've done it all
wrong, never stirring
easily toward the available light
with the confidence and stamina
it knows.

THE DANDELION

The unreadable face of the dandelion
turns sideways or forward
toward possible moonlight or sunlight,
each golden circle of fibers
looks like the yellow star
on people's overcoats,
1938.

THE COLOR YELLOW

A yellow light
floats above the houses
this autumn. Sour apple
smells ride the air.
Seagulls suspend
the color over the river,
claiming the updraft
and the downdraft.
Cottonwoods pump yellow
blood through their veins.
The sun makes citrus drinks
of the late dandelions.
Even the grass turns lemon
on the overheated plain.
We feed the pale ending
of summer to our eyes,
a child's color,
painted with fingers
on paper clouds.

CAFÉ NO SÉ

I find Café No Sé in yellow plaster.
The women cook meat in front
on small dark grills,
spreading guacamole on everything.

A long parade of orange, yellow, purple plants
tumbles over the rooftops,
and again, I'm lost,
wandering loosely through the avenidas,
going south or north, I can't say.

What a surprise to discover a street more quiet
and green than the last.
Never find yourself loose and lost.
You never find yourself until you are lost,
and the lavender trees sweep over the sky
disguised as the sky.
The yellow flowers creep
easily over yellow plaster.

I find Café I Don't Know
after traveling the Spanish grid,
mazing the corners and chipped citrus walls.
Some landmarks among landmarks
all look the same.

Happiness

Button up
and keep it all a secret
in this cold world,
this little thing we have
that no one suspects
because we are married and silent.

Let them laugh out loud
if they want to release something.
We'll keep on holding hands
when it's forty below outside,
and the gray sky has nothing good to say
to the shivering bark of a young tree.
Your skin will be tender as a child's
under the rough, gloved hand.

CONSOLATION PRIZE

Flabbergasted
as he was
by fate and luck
and the quick draw of the shorter
stick time after time,
he was finally content
with his love
and his dwelling place
of stucco and grass, the true
colors in her eyes
glowing like the sky
in sharp blues,
and taking
it all in simply
everyday
kept him in roses.

RAY BRADBURY STANDING

An afternoon sun flushes the curtain red and pushes the room toward a warm remoteness. I am wishing to be at the right hand of God among colorific saints and angels when Jesus Christ enters the room and stands in the sunlight. He is wearing a dark suit and I am immediately aware that it is the very suit Ray Bradbury wore to his high school graduation ceremony—the suit that Ray's uncle was shot in during an armed robbery. I don't believe it is Jesus in Ray Bradbury's graduation suit until I put my finger in the bullet hole.

PORTRAIT

Hungry and lost
like a dog in the street,
he reads the dark pavement,
sniffs the dirt and grass.
He knows decay and new growth,
the scent of evening trees.
The comforts they give
are like the warm silence of sleep.
He's been kicked and ignored,
promised better food.
And still, a restlessness
keeps him awake.
He circles the city park,
inhales the last of the flowers.
He makes his own bones happy.

Epitaph

Here lies the mailman,
weary of his route,
still afraid of dogs, snow,
and lost delivery.

THE PRACTICE

In the diminishing light
of October,
we watch the trees go to sleep.
The crows are hidden
in clouds, and the sparrows
are silent.
We listen for other endings:
the whimpering rain on the roof,
the constant drop of pine needles
falling on themselves.
Our minds are full of twigs and ashes,
and the cold rain that is called joy.
We take pleasure in these small deaths.
We watch,
we practice.

IN THE LOBBY OF THE AFTERLIFE

We'll all sit together in the holding room
inside a clean Howard Johnson.
Friendly ones, loud ones,
and complete strangers
will all be as one.
People with laptops and nice hair
will sit among us in the cheerful comfort
of Naugahyde chairs, eating gratis
peanuts and feeling a little anxious
about what is
to come.

THE DEAD

All those who died
still shuffle among us
with their gray beards and piercing eyes.
Their boats still float in the lagoon,
their white canes lean on the back door.
A thousand pairs of glasses
rest on the desks of the vanquished.
Their plants still grow, their e-mails
still tremble on old computers.
We hear them coming and going
down the darkened hallways.
We see them move in the corners of our eyes.
They are figures without substance,
people who possess neither time
nor dignity, but live on in the narrow
and heated rooms of love and memory.

FAITH

We try to pull the veil
over the eyes of the gods.
We say we are humble
but walk the streets in shadows,
wanting to trust something beyond this crusty
snow, that dying animal.
The wind is deceptive too, and tells
lies to the bark on the trees.
Our hearts are bruised and weak,
worrying ruts in the carpet.
We refuse to ask for assistance
from lovers or friends.
We hear the low voice
of our own sorrows
asking the trees for a dance.

DISCOVERING PERIWINKLE

Blue flowering vine, name unknown,
St. Francis lives underneath.
Cirrus clouds race overhead, while the wind argues
with one of its branches.

The vine is almost still
when the sun fades at four o'clock.
An insect crawls through,
and I notice tendrils that are dead, brittle,
holding some darkness against the garden wall.
The light blue droppings stain the grass.

Days here in the courtyard, under the spell
of star blossoms, have been good.
I will miss the five-pointed kindness,
the blue surprises.
If the sun catches these lavender facets again,
I'll live in the color of the sky,
and count all the petals and glories.

photo by Judy Triese

Carol Rucks grew up in a large family in Central Wisconsin. She was educated at the University of Wisconsin, Stevens Point, where she studied literature and creative writing with David Steingass and Dave Engel. She has traveled widely in Eastern and Western Europe and in Latin America. She studied poetry writing with Rosann Lloyd in Guatemala, as part of Art Workshops in Guatemala. She has worked mainly in libraries, including the Golda Meir Library in Milwaukee, and also the Art/Music/Literature Department of the Minneapolis Central Library, which later became part of the Hennepin County Library system.

Her poems have appeared in *Abraxas, Energy Review, Colere, West Branch, Dust and Fire,* and elsewhere. She is actively involved with the Loft Literary Center and its classes and readings, and was a finalist in the Loft Mentor Series for 2012. She lives in Minneapolis with her husband, Mark McHugh.